Mweru Wantipa National Park

Lake Tanganyika

Lake Mweru

Lake Mweru Wantipa

• Mbala

TANZANIA

Sumbu National Park

Lusenga Plain National Park

• Kawambwa

150    200   Kilometres

• Luwingu

• KASAMA

Isoka •

*Chambeshi*

Nyika National Park

ZAIRE

*Luapula*

Lake Bangwelu

MANSA •

• Samfya

Isangano National Park

• Nyika

MALAWI

SOLWEZI •

Mpika •

North Luangwa National Park

Chililabombwe •

Lavushi Manda
National Park

Chingola •

• Mufulira

• Lundazi

Kalulushi •

• KITWE

Luanshya •

• NDOLA

South Luangwa
National Park

Lukusuzi National Park

npa •

*Kafue*

• Serenje

• Mkushi

*Luangwa*

CHIPATA •

Kapiri Mposhi •

• Katete

Mita  Hills Dam

Petauke •

KABWE •

Mulungushi  Dam

Mumbwa •

*Lusemfwa*

MOZAMBIQUE

Blue Lagoon
National Park

• Rufunsa

Park

■ LUSAKA

Lower Zambezi National Park

-Tezhi

Namwala •

• Mazabuka

ochinvar National Park

• Chirundu

• Monze

• Siavonga

obezi

• Choma

Lake Kariba

Kalomo •

ZIMBABWE

• Sinazongwe

a National Park

LIVINGSTONE

LS

# ZAMBIA

*Photographs by Ian Murphy*
*Text edited by Richard Vaughan*

*ISBN No. 9515209 0 3*

**Publisher**
*CBC Publishing*
*50 Kaguvi Street, Harare, Zimbabwe*
*Telephone  ++ 263- 4 - 750205*

**Design**
*Pilcher Graphics Limited*
*25 Joseph Mwila Road, Rhodes Park*
*Lusaka, Zambia*
*Telephone  ++ 260 - 1 - 211695*

**Imagesetting**
*HPP Studios*
*Fidelity Life Tower*
*Raleigh Street, Harare, Zimbabwe*
*Telephone ++ 263 - 4 - 756873*

**Printing & binding**
*Tien Wah Press (PTE) Limited*
*977 Bukit Timah Road*
*Singapore 2158*

*Photographs are available for commercial usage from:*
*Tony Stone Worldwide*
*116 - 134 Bayham Street*
*London NW1 OBA, UK*
*Telephone  ++44 - 171 - 267 - 8988*

*In memory of my Father*

*For*
*Andy, Caroline, Odette and Murray Anderson*
*Mick, Joan, Rosie and Nathan Pilcher*

*This edition has been made possible by the kind assistance of Mr. Bill Irwin*
*Managing Director of the Standard Chartered Bank of Zambia Limited*

*Previous page Nyika Plateau*

# Contents

# Introduction

This is a picture book. More than that, it is a visual essay which attempts to capture the beauty and diversity of one of the lesser known states in Africa. The Republic of Zambia, tucked away in the centre of the continent, has not captured the world's imagination with the same success as some of her neighbours. Zimbabwe, Tanzania and Kenya all attract more foreign visitors and are better covered in the Western media. But in spite of her comparative obscurity, Zambia has a great deal to offer: the country is spacious, varied, unspoilt in many areas - and has been politically stable for the last twenty years.

On the map, Zambia is shown as a huge, lopsided butterfly, lying across the heart of the interior plateau of southern Africa. It covers three quarters of a million square kilometres - as much as France, Switzerland, Austria and Hungary combined. Since the plateau on which it rests is over a kilometre above sea level, the climate is warm but not humid, and amongst the most pleasant the world can offer.

The population of Zambia is about eight million, the great majority of her people coming from the Bantu group. But Zambia is also home to small numbers from many other ethnic backgrounds - not least the British, who colonised the country, and whose language is used for education, commerce and law.

Zambia's physical situation makes it a difficult country to run. Its highly irregular shape is a legacy of the colonial era, when Europeans divided the spoils of Africa to meet their own interests. As a result, internal communication is difficult and the borders hard to patrol. To complicate her affairs further, the country is surrounded by no less than eight neighbours. Even more telling is the fact that Zambia is landlocked: her economic heartland is more than a thousand kilometres from the sea at the nearest point. Large sectors of the economy hang on slender transport lifelines, including the export of copper, which is Zambia's biggest earner of foreign exchange.

## The First Zambians

Signs of human habitation in Zambia go back some two hundred thousand years. At the small town of Mbala in the far north of the country, there is evidence of layer upon layer of occupation covering half this period. These earliest Zambians lived by gathering fruits, hunting wild animals and possibly fishing.

Eventually they learnt to make simple wooden clubs and spears. They also discovered how to make fire, the charred logs and ash at Kalambo being the earliest evidence of its use in Sub-Saharan Africa. These people are divided from modern man most significantly by their failure to produce food by tilling the soil and planting seeds. That great leap was not made until about fifteen hundred years ago, when iron-working, cattle herding and farming people began to move into Zambia from the north.

They were unlike the small Bushmen they displaced, being larger in stature, and they spoke an early form of Bantu language. They came in such large numbers that within a few hundred years, the Stone Age Bush people had almost entirely disappeared.

The country in which the newcomers found themselves was much as it is today - a great sea of woodland in which they cleared space for their huts and crops. They lived in villages as kinsmen of the same clan, and usually married outside into other clans. They believed in a High God, the creator of all things, including spirits of the earth and sky, and spirits of the clan's ancestors. They also believed in magic and witchcraft, and in the use of charms to bring success in love, war and hunting.

The most important institution of government for these people was through chiefs: some of them were mere headmen of villages while others ruled like kings over great areas, and were regarded as almost divine. It is from the ceremonials of chiefly succession that Zambia's oral traditions grew, providing much of the evidence for the way of life that endured for several centuries until the strangers came.

Until the eighteenth century, Africa was valued only for its gold, ivory and slaves. Zambia, in the far interior, was remote from the sea coast and, with the exception of the area around Feira, from the influence of either the Arabs or the Portuguese who dominated the trade in these commodities. But as the demand increased for slaves to service sugar plantations in Brazil, so did Portuguese penetration into Africa.

For centuries, trade in the interior had been conducted not by money but by barter. The simple range of everyday commodities - salt, ironwork, pottery, cloth, cosmetics - were exchanged between groups adept at fulfilling the need for each of them. Now this became disrupted by the demand for ivory. African ivory is softer than Indian, and it was Indian carvers who wanted it.

Copper, too, was in demand. At this time, it was wanted simply for decoration and ornaments. Much of it was imported, but there were important early mines in Zambia: at Kanshanshi it had been mined from the fifth century, and at Bwana Mkubwa the ancient workings were a kilometre long and fifty metres deep in places. But it was gold, not copper, which brought the Portuguese to Zumbo on the east bank of the Zambezi, and the earliest recorded settlement was in 1546. In 1732, they opened a trading post and called it Feira, the market. At the height of the post's activity, copper was passing through from Feira to Zumbo in tonnes every year, and elephant tusks went by the hundred.

It was a very different stranger who brought the greatest change to Zambia. David Livingstone, the son of a poor Scottish mill-worker, qualified as a doctor by grim hard work and joined the London Missionary Society. In 1841, he arrived in southern Africa. The missionaries, of whom Livingstone was one, were a formidable body of men and women. They were earnest, tough, and filled with unshakeable conviction. Livingstone had in addition a passionate inquisitiveness, and after nine frustrating years he could not resist setting off with his family across the Kalahari Desert, into the unknown. On their third expedition in June 1851, Livingstone was in his own words, "rewarded by the discovery of the Zambezi in the centre of the continent." As a missionary and explorer, he endured years of hardship and privation, travelling countless miles on foot, engaged in constant scientific observation and copious writings. "Fear God and work hard," he always told his children.

When he came to England in 1856 after an absence of sixteen years, Livingstone found himself a national hero. In his most famous lecture, delivered to an excited audience packed in the Senate House of Cambridge University, he ended with a shout:

"I beg to direct your attention to Africa. I know that in a few years I shall be cut off in that country, which is now open. Do not let it be shut again! I go back to Africa to try to make a path for commerce and Christianity. Do carry on the work which I have begun. I leave it with you ! "

Livingstone became caught up in the prevailing obsession with finding the source of the Nile. His sixtieth birthday on March 19th, 1873, found him struggling desperately through the marshes of Lake Bangweulu, dying slowly from the haemorrhages brought on by years of dysentery. At the village of Chief Chitambo, he was laid gently on a litter of sticks and grass, where he fell into a terminal coma. "Knocked up quite," said the last entry in his diary. Some time before dawn on May 1st 1873, Livingstone made a last supreme effort and fell to his knees beside his rough bed. There, his faithful companions, Susi and Chuma, found him dead. They buried his heart under a tree at Chitambo's village, dried and wrapped his body, and in a feat of great endurance, marched it a thousand miles to the coast, whence it was taken by ship to London. On 18 April 1874, Livingstone was buried at Westminster Abbey.

Livingstone's main achievement was to arouse British missionary interest in the territory north of the Zambezi. He had been convinced that the industrial power of Britain and the expansion of British trade were essential to the working out of the Divine Plan, and he believed that Africans would only be persuaded to accept the Christian gospel if their social and economic conditions were improved. For Livingstone, this meant learning new skills from European advisers and growing crops for export to Europe. The great obstacle to such progress was the slave trade, but Livingstone was sure that this would slowly disappear once slavers were given an opportunity to profit by more legitimate activities.

## Britain Takes Over

Ten years after Livingstone's death, the colonial powers sat down in Berlin, the Prussian capital, and marked a map with boundaries of their spheres of influence in Africa. The actual borders of their territories were drawn later, but by the turn of the century, the physical shape of the colonies had been decided, creating the ethnic and geographical anomalies that have plagued the continent ever since.

From 1885 onwards, more and more Europeans entered southern Africa to make good the territorial claims of their governments. African and Arab slave traders, many of whom had in the past shown friendship towards individual missionaries and explorers, now felt threatened. As a result, the next three decades saw the region plunged into intense conflict: slavers fought to preserve their livelihood, while the European powers vied with each other to claim the most attractive slices of land.

In economic terms Livingstone's journeys had born little fruit. It was only reports of his last wanderings and the inspiring tale of his death which sparked a resurgence of missionary interest in central Africa. Nonetheless by 1884, when the Berlin Conference took place, the British missionary presence north of the Zambezi was sufficient for her to have the strongest claim on the territory.

Missionaries had reported back to Europe on the slave trade which still flourished in the region. Slavers like Msiri and Tippu Tip made huge fortunes in human flesh, and staked out large tracts of land to facilitate their operations. But the missionaries also informed the European world that Katanga, part of Msiri's domain, was rich in copper. Thus, the region quickly became a focus for secular interests.

British economic activity further south had been vigorous. Diamonds had been discovered at Kimberley in South Africa, and attracted the interest of a young entrepreneur called Cecil Rhodes. He had come out from England to improve his health, but he soon did much more. By 1880, when he was only twenty-seven, he and his partners in De Beers dominated the diamond industry. Through De Beers, Rhodes obtained complete control of Kimberley in 1888, and his wealth broadened his ambitions: he wanted to see the British flag fly the length of Africa, from the Cape to Cairo.

A year later he managed to persuade the British government to grant a charter to the new company he had formed - the British South Africa Company. This allowed Rhodes to use the authority of the British government in staking out claims to African territory at the expense of other European nations. In the north, Rhodes confronted three European powers: the Portuguese in Angola and Mozambique, the Germans in East Africa, and the newly formed Congo Free State of the Belgian King Leopold II.

The Germans were easily contained. In 1889, treaties with the Mambwe, Lungu and Tabwa chiefs between Lakes Malawi and Tanganyika effectively sealed them off. A year later Rhodes sent three expeditions to forestall the advances of Leopold and the Portuguese in the territory north of the Zambezi as far as Katanga. All were instructed to make treaties with chiefs which would grant British aid and 'protection', in return for pledges from the chiefs not to make agreements with any other Europeans. The territories thus secured gave Britain control over all the land to the west of Lake Malawi and east of Katanga. In 1891, a treaty forced on Portugal finally dashed her hopes of uniting her territories of Angola in the west and Mozambique in the east.

As for Leopold and Katanga, this question was effectively settled the same year. Two expeditions, one working for Rhodes, the other for Leopold, reached Msiri's capital almost at the same time. The British envoy who arrived first failed to get a concession from Msiri. The expedition for Leopold had a violent argument with Msiri and one of its agents - ironically a British officer - shot him dead. Suddenly Leopold's men found themselves in command of Msiri's kingdom. British claims on the territory evaporated, and in 1894 a treaty between Leopold and the British government granted him the so-called "Pedicle", a long arm of territory which reached deep into the company's sphere.

In 1899 Company administration was imposed, and on 17 August 1911, the two halves of the territory, almost cut off from one another by the Pedicle, were united to form the single province of Northern Rhodesia. Its borders define the modern state of Zambia, and account for its bizarre and disjointed shape.

The danger of slavery at the hands of the Arabs was replaced by a colonial system, with power firmly residing in a small group of British officers. Rhodes himself had died in 1902 at the age of 49, but the British South Africa Company lived on. Northern Rhodesia was in effect a "Company state". The significance of this was not immediately apparent to most Africans. The Company's first officials and soldiers had gained entry by talking to a small number of chiefs, and they had often been welcomed as a source of protection against local African enemies. The British had engaged in some fighting, but hardly on a larger scale than the skirmishes which were endemic in much of the country. The full significance of Company rule did not become clear until it had set up a local administration, and begun collecting tax. It was this above all which finally convinced the ordinary villager that both he and his chief had a new master.

At first, Northern Rhodesia was a poor country. Many of the known copper reserves were in the Congo Free State, and fertile topsoil was scarce. Besides, the world was not interested in the prospect of agricultural products being eked out on long supply lines from central Africa. Instead, it wanted men. Thirty years earlier as the European powers busied themselves carving up central Africa, gold was being discovered on the Rand. Now, parties of Gwembe, Tonga, Lozi and Toka were going south. For the subjects of Northern Rhodesia the future meant migration, to sell their labour in distant farms, towns and mines.

Mining in the state itself was not even covering the administrative costs of Company rule. When in 1924, formal political control was passed to the Crown, making Northern Rhodesia a British Protectorate, the British South Africa Company retained the country's mineral rights. But these seemed of little value - Rhodes' dream of a new Witwatersrand in the north had not been fulfilled.

In the years following the transfer of power, world demand for copper began to escalate. More intense prospecting revealed huge orebodies in the Copperbelt where none had been suspected. Britain responded by strengthening the institutions of the colonial administration, servicing the mining industry, supporting the white commercial farmers and facilitating the growth of towns.

The Company had done little for the African people by way of education or health provision, and the British administration did not improve on this substantially in the early years. Instead money was invested in capital equipment. Mining had to be carried out deep underground, requiring expensive plant development and construction. Highly capitalised companies developed, dominated by Rhodesian Anglo American (Rhoanglo) and the Rhodesian Selection Trust (RST).

Because the mining companies were formally domiciled in London until 1950, they paid their taxes to the British government and not to the local administration inside Northern Rhodesia. At the same time, they had to pay royalties to the British South

Africa Company. This meant that the funds were not available for local expenditure, and the indigenous Africans were the first to suffer as a result. In the mines, racial discrimination was practiced in matters of pay and employment and after a while, industrial unrest was inevitable.

The first attempt to deal with African workers' grievances was the appointment of tribal representatives, elders of each tribal group who attended monthly discussions with management. It was an experiment which survived until 1953, but it was not really appropriate to the problems of industrial employment. In the words of Lawrence Katilungu, pioneer trade unionist, "The traditional medium of African administration had lost its impact in an urban setting."

In 1935, as the celebrations King George's silver jubilee reached their climax with the removal of the capital from Livingstone to Lusaka, a crisis was building up on the Copperbelt. The government ill-advisedly changed the basis of tax assessment without warning, reducing it in the country districts and raising it in the towns. There was no consultation, and the Copperbelt's first strikes began in May. The elders proved of little assistance. Strikes turned to riots, troops were flown in, and at Luanshya six men were killed. The subsequent commission of inquiry led to the appointment of a labour advisory board and eventually to the establishment of a government labour department.

The strike had shown the potential strength of African miners. By this time many were clearly showing a capacity to take over jobs reserved for Europeans, who formed the Northern Rhodesia Mine Workers Union (NRMWU) in order to safeguard their interests against their fellow workers as much as their employers. Early in 1940 the NRMWU organised strikes at Mufulira and Nkana in protest against the rise in the cost of living brought about by the war in Europe, and its claims were largely conceded. This success at once stimulated the Africans to make claims of their own. In April the same year, they staged a strike at Nkana which lasted for a week and then came to a bloody end. Strikers threw stones at fellow-workers suspected of strike-breaking; soldiers began shooting and seventeen strikers were killed.

## The Nationalist Movement

Under this climate, nationalist sentiments gained strength, but because so few Africans at the time could read and write, modern-style politics were slow to emerge. In fact the early nationalist movement owed much to Africans in neighbouring Nyasaland, for it was here that education had advanced much further. From the beginning of the century, 'Nyasas' had occupied many of the semi-skilled jobs which were open to Africans in Northern Rhodesia.

David Kaunda was one of them. Trained at the famous Livingstonia Mission, he was sent westward in 1905 into what is now Zambia's Northern Province to preach among the Bemba people. In 1923, he formed a welfare association at Mwenzo in the far north of the country. Its aims included "helpful means of developing the country in the hands of the two necessary connecting links - the government and the governed". But its membership never grew and it disappeared in 1928.

1930 saw the foundation of a number of welfare associations along the line of rail. Their activities seldom ventured into politics, and an attempt to form a United African Welfare Association of Northern Rhodesia (1933) failed. It was on the Copperbelt, where labour conditions were particularly hard, that African protest first became organised.

The Second World War provided an opportunity for many Zambians to travel widely in the armed forces, and to return to their homeland with their political awareness heightened. In 1946, a conference was held in Lusaka for representatives of workers' welfare societies. The result was the Federation of Welfare Societies, which dealt not only with urban and industrial grievances but broader political issues as well. One prominent member of the Federation was Kenneth Kaunda, David's son. In 1948, the Federation reformed itself as the Northern Rhodesia Congress, the first political party for Africans. At the same time, Britain began to introduce greater political responsibility for Africans in her colonies, and she dispatched a trade union adviser to the Copperbelt. In 1949, the Northern Rhodesia African Mine Workers' Trade Union was formed. African representation on the Nyasaland and Northern Rhodesia Legislative Councils began in 1948, so that by 1953 there were three African members on the Nyasaland Council and four on the Northern Rhodesia Council. The same trend appeared in local government: Urban Advisory Councils were created, and all African Town Management Boards were set up on the Copperbelt.

Since the 1930s, the European minority in Northern Rhodesia had been growing increasingly worried about their future. Some European politicians, chief among whom was Roy Welensky, wanted amalgamation of the two Rhodesias in order to preserve European rule.

The British Government responded by insisting on federation rather than amalgamation, and on the inclusion of the poorer territory of Nyasaland as well. There were obvious advantages for both North and South in this. For the North it meant political support from the much larger white minority south of the Zambezi: for the South, it meant the prospect of shared profits from the Copperbelt.

African leaders opposed the idea from the outset, seeing it as a means of preserving European domination indefinitely. In spite of their protests, plans for the Federation went ahead. In 1951 it was discussed by colonial officials in London and a conference was called at the Victoria Falls, to which African representatives were invited. They boycotted the meeting, preferring instead to make known their opposition to the whole idea.

In spite of their protests, the Federation of Rhodesia and Nyasaland came into being in October 1953. Its constitution was designed to preserve racial imbalance in political affairs, so that of the thirty-five seats in the new parliament, only six were reserved for Africans, and there was no extension of the franchise to increase the proportion. Over the ten year lifetime of the Federation, the African population gained little from it. More European settlers arrived, the colour bar persisted and living conditions hardly improved.

As time went by it became clear that Southern Rhodesia was benefiting more from the new arrangement than her partners. Large grants from federal funds went to the setting up of new industries in the south. A particularly telling blow came in 1955, when the Federal Government announced without prior consultation that the new Zambezi hydro-electric plant would be sited at Kariba on the southern side of the river. Both in Northern Rhodesia and Nyasaland, politicians began to have serious doubts about the Federation.

In 1956, Roy Welensky became Federal Prime Minister. It was clear to all that under his leadership, Africans could not hope for an improvement in their lot. The African Congresses now had to fight for every advance, and nationalist leaders became more militant. When in 1958, a British government white paper outlining moderate changes to the Northern Rhodesia Legislative Council was issued, Harry Nkumbula treated it to a public burning. The Northern Rhodesia Congress split in two, and the more radical of the groups became the Zambia African National Congress, under the leadership of Kenneth Kaunda.

By 1959 a state of emergency had been declared in Nyasaland and Southern Rhodesia, following the unfounded rumours that the Nyasaland African Congress was about to launch a 'murder plot' against Europeans. As a result, the ZANC was banned and several of its leaders - including Kaunda himself - were sent to gaol. This kind of repression only stiffened African resistance. A new party was formed, the United National Independence Party (UNIP). In January 1960, Kaunda was released from gaol and discovered that he had become a popular hero. The leadership of UNIP naturally fell into his hands.

By now, the Federation was creaking. Its own constitution required that its progress be reviewed seven to nine years after its introduction. This review was preceded by an advisory commission under one of Britain's most distinguished lawyers, Lord Monckton. To the horror of the Federal Government its report, published in 1960, recommended that "the strength of African opposition in the Northern territories is such that the Federation cannot, in our view, be maintained in its present form."

As the political situation became more tense, violence was inevitable. Any move towards greater political freedom for the majority was fiercely opposed by Roy Welensky and the settlers. But pressure towards liberalisation was now coming from another quarter. Britain was rapidly shedding her empire, which had become economically and morally untenable. Of the sub-Saharan states, Ghana and Nigeria were already independent, while Uganda, Kenya, Tanzania and several other states were well on the way.

In 1961 Britain had talks with UNIP and proposed a new, liberal constitution, but Welensky and his colleagues persuaded the British government to drop the idea. In July that year, UNIP's leader Kenneth Kaunda pulled off a resounding personal triumph. Speaking to 4,000 delegates at the historic Mulungushi Conference, he launched an impassioned attack on the British and Federal Governments. Pledging himself to "strike at the very roots of the British Government in this country", Kaunda claimed that UNIP would wage "practical, non-violent war" against the Federation until it was completely destroyed and Africans ruled Northern Rhodesia.

The European minority was forced to allow political reform. The Federation withered and disappeared at the end of 1963, and a new constitution for Northern Rhodesia was devised. Elections in January 1964 gave UNIP a substantial majority on the Legislative Council, and the new government rapidly negotiated independence with Britain. Nine months later, the Republic of Zambia was born.

The handover was a peaceful affair, attended by thousands of all races at a huge Independence Stadium outside Lusaka. At two minutes to midnight on Friday 23rd October 1964, the military parade presented arms and the British National Anthem was played for the last time. The stadium lights were extinguished, the Union Jack and the standard of the last governor, Sir Evelyn Hone, were lowered. One minute before the hour, a fanfare was sounded by trumpeters of the massed bands, and at the moment of midnight, a single spotlight shone on the flag of the Republic of Zambia which was slowly raised as the Zambian National Anthem was played. The next day, the Princess Royal handed to Kenneth Kaunda the Constitutional Instruments which brought Zambia into being.

## Independence

Zambia was one of the last African countries to throw off the colonial yoke. For many fledgling states, independence meant little in economic terms, because African resources so often remained in the hands of interests overseas. In Zambia the problem was particularly acute, because she depended so heavily on one commodity - copper - and had failed to diversify her activities.

World demand for copper was bound to fluctuate, and under colonial rule the industry had been an enclave of foreign business. The mines exported copper as a raw material, without any processing for domestic use. At the same time, inputs for industry and services were imported, leaving little scope for the emergence of an indigenous industrial base.

Agriculture was the other potential breadwinner, and this was firmly in the control of white farmers. Consequently there was little scope for the emergence of African entre-preneurs - the lack of financial security for small business blocked many entries to urban trading and other routes to capital accumulation. The British South Africa Company's surrender of its mineral rights on the eve of Independence Day was a major step towards economic self-sufficiency, but there was another, purely geographical factor which worked against the young republic's fortunes.

Because she was landlocked in central Africa, Zambia had to rely on Rhodesia, South Africa, Mozambique and Angola for nearly all her communications with the outside world. All Zambia's coal and coke came from Wankie, much of her electrical power came from the Kariba hydro-electric station on the south bank of the Zambezi, and her main lines of access to the sea were through Rhodesia to Mozambique or South Africa. At the time of Independence, Zambia depended on Rhodesia for sixty per cent of all her imports.

In November 1965 Rhodesia's Prime Minister, Ian Smith, unilaterally declared Rhodesia's independence, preferring to maintain white supremacy in an isolated republic than succumb to British pressure for reform. Britain responded with economic sanctions, naively believing that these would swiftly undermine Smith's regime.

But Rhodesia's links with the outside world were also Zambia's, and she was affected by the sanctions too. In particular, the closure of the oil pipeline from Beira to Rhodesia was a major blow. At first, oil was flown into the country at huge expense, then it was hauled two thousand kilometres over a dirt road from Dar es Salaam in Tanzania. At the same time, copper had to be exported through Dar in the east and the Angolan port of Lobito in the west. Eventually a major railway was built with the help of China, which linked the Copperbelt with Dar by 1975.

Economic difficulties were complemented by social problems. Before Independence, racial discrimination and legal colour bars prevented Africans from rising within the civil service, army and police. There were hardly any African army or police officers, judges or senior managers, and few Africans ever rose in status above head clerk. Zambia had probably suffered the worst colonial neglect in the field of education. On the eve of Independence, there were less than 100 university graduates, one lawyer, one engineer, two doctors, and only 961 Africans with Cambridge school certificates available to the new UNIP government. Among these, African women were almost entirely absent.

## The Philosophy of Humanism

The rigid system of race domination which preceded him explains the political programme adopted by President Kaunda. The proclaimed goal was African democratic socialism, which would bring liberation from undemocratic, imperial and colonial rule, abolish race discrimination, help African traders in commerce, and take other measures to introduce a more egalitarian society.

'Humanism' became Zambia's national philosophy, conceived as a creed which harked back to the social values of traditional Zambian society before western industrialisation. Equality of opportunity, respect for the elderly under the extended family system, and loyalty to the young republic were all central to the new code of conduct.

A mood of optimism surged through the country, fanned by the steadily rising price of copper on the international market. In the first six years of Independence, there was a sevenfold increase in government revenue. Employment was increased in the state sector, wages rose substantially, social services were extended, and credits made for African farmers and businessmen. While the living standards of the majority improved only slightly, there were visible benefits to most people in health services and education.

Yet the men who exercised political authority knew that their power in many areas was limited. This was because much control still lay with decision makers in the mining companies and other multinationals dominating the economy, and not with government. Decisions on prices, subsidies, wage levels and transport were frequently referred to these private interests, since any wrong move could easily destabilise such a highly concentrated economy. Also it was clear that much of the profit from mining was being syphoned abroad, and President Kaunda's first five year plan urged the rapid development of agriculture as an alternative.

In the event, little progress was made as the economy continued to be dominated by the needs of copper and the foreign corporations who controlled it. In a further effort to combat this, the 'Mulungushi reforms' of 1968 sought to encourage the emergence of African businessmen by restricting retail trade outside the towns and small building contracts to Zambian citizens. The government took a majority share in many retail stores and building supply firms, as well as two major breweries. In the next three years, the government took over 51 per cent of share capital in twenty four large private foreign companies. The Zambian state became one of the most interventionist in the Third World.

The policy of replacing expatriates with Zambians markedly affected the country's demography. Many white expatriates left when their jobs were handed over to Africans. Thus, the economy was no longer sharply divided on racial lines: instead, a rift grew between the black people of the towns and those of the country.

The overwhelming predominance of the copper industry meant that economic development continued to be concentrated around the Copperbelt and the towns along the railway line down the middle of the country: by contrast, the development of agriculture was so slow that rural poverty remained an acute problem.

In order to maintain a delicate balance between intervention on the one hand and selling out to foreign interests on the other, President Kaunda's government rapidly built a system of state corporations called parastatals, which were state owned and organised within a single corporate structure. The Boards of these institutions had a majority of Zambians appointed by the state to look after their interests, but they remained isolated entities, engaged in the kind of import substitution that often meant a reliance on foreign inputs and expatriate personnel. In short, nationalisation did not necessarily lead to development.

Crucially, manufacturing was not in a position to use indigenous raw materials, nor did it aim to supply consumer goods for the rural people. It was a purely urban affair. Hence, the gap between town and country grew steadily, making the economy even more distorted than it had been under colonial rule.

A rural exodus began, as people from the countryside came to the cities to look for work. Because many of the white people in higher positions had now left, a new African class emerged, a class of well-heeled bureaucrats, industrialists and government officials.

In spite of efforts to diversify the economy, Zambia remained heavily dependent on copper for foreign exchange throughout the 1970's. When the world's economy slowed down copper prices fell sharply, and the country rapidly developed an external deficit which became an intolerable burden. Zambia became an IMF 'patient' in 1973, long before most other countries. The IMF provided several successive short term loans, which only increased long term indebtedness. Zambia found she was struggling to pay the interest on the debt, let alone the capital itself.

As the country's economic situation deteriorated, political stability was becoming increasingly threatened by the war in Rhodesia to the south. Kaunda's government was inevitably sympathetic to the guerrillas who were fighting the government of Premier Ian Smith which denied universal franchise on the grounds of colour. A result was that the border along the Zambezi was closed for everything except copper exports. These were subsequently diverted along much more protracted routes to the outside world, precipitating a further decline in the economy. At the same time, international copper prices dropped, forcing import restrictions and widespread discontent among the local population.

Within UNIP, there was serious disagreement over the way to handle Rhodesia, given the extent to which Zambia's economic fortunes depended on good supply lines to and from the south. In October 1978 rail links were restored and an agreement was reached on shipping exports via South Africa. But by this time Zambia had been openly harbouring members of the Zimbabwe African Peoples' Union (ZAPU), causing the Smith regime to launch pre-emptive attacks within Zambia's borders, including two air attacks on Lusaka itself.

The situation was only diffused after Zimbabwe's independence in 1980, but although an economic recovery was expected, conditions for most Zambians only got worse. A coup attempt which took place in October that year was blamed by Kaunda on South Africa, but many of those arrested after the incident turned out to be ethnic Bemba, traditional opponents of the President.

Despite his introduction of harsh austerity measures, Kaunda retained strong grassroots support. In October 1983 he was re-elected leader, receiving, as sole candidate, 93 per cent of the votes cast, compared with 81 per cent in 1978. Throughout the 1980s, however, Zambia suffered continuing economic privation amid charges of corruption and inefficiency in high places. The abrupt replacement of expatriate labour after independence with unskilled locals was making itself felt in both the public and private sectors, to the extent that the traditional divide in prosperity between the territories north and south of the Zambezi had become a painful one.

In the rest of the world the political climate was changing on two fronts. To the north, Mikhail Gorbachev implemented reforms in the moribund Soviet communist system which were eventually to seal its fate, paving the way for the disintegration of the Soviet Union and its replacement by a motley collection of disoriented post-communist states. The repercussions were felt across Eastern Europe, culminating in the demolition of the Berlin Wall and the liberation of millions from 50 years of tyranny. Gorbachev himself had planted the seeds of his own destruction, and was swept away by the ebullience of Boris Yeltsin.

In South Africa, President Frederick de Klerk moved cautiously towards electoral reform, prodded on by international sanctions which were seriously undermining the economy. Demands for Nelson Mandela's release became irresistible. The Afrikaner leaders knew, as they had known all along, that Mandela's release would end the apartheid era, which is exactly what it did. De Klerk's task was to negotiate the reform process in such a way as to keep change as peaceful as possible, and in this he had a good measure of success.

The implications of these developments for countries like Zambia were far-reaching. Eastern Europe was suddenly an attractive place for western investors and donors who had traditionally been frustrated by their experiences in post-colonial Africa, and in particular by the skill of African leaders in manipulating West against East to take financial and other advantage from Cold War politics.

However, the ending of the Cold War and the advancement of human rights in South Africa could now enable pressure for reform to be transferred to those one-party states north of the Limpopo which had been acceptable simply because they had been opposed to communism. Pressure was now brought to bear on African states to liberalise their economies and to focus development through multi-party democracies. Throughout Africa, advocates of reform took up the cause of multi-partyism.

## The Arrival of Multi-party Democracy

It is to Kaunda's credit that in 1991, although he said Zambia was "not ready" for multi-party politics, he did not block the reform process. In fact, the President had seriously misread the mood of the electorate and he was visibly shocked when he and his party were swept from office by the rival Movement for Multi-party Democracy (MMD) led by Frederick Chiluba. The MMD won 125 seats in the national assembly compared with UNIP's 25. Only four members of the previous government were returned.

Once in office, President Chiluba's primary task was to introduce a Structural Adjustment Programme (SAP) sponsored by the International Monetary Fund and the World Bank. It has been a painful process. By the time Chiluba took office Zambia had declined economically from being one of the most prosperous countries in Sub-Saharan Africa to one of the poorest in the world, with a GNP per capita of only US$290. The underlying causes of this were failures of public policy and governance. In addition, all key sectors of the economy were in the hands of some 130 parastatal companies, most of which were poorly managed.

After the process of Zambianisation, which was intended to transform Zambia into a modern industrial state under the philosophy of humanism, the country went on a consumption binge which only stopped when the healthy reserves left by the departing British at independence had been depleted. The oil shocks of the early 1970s impacted on an economy no longer able to absorb them, the price of copper, Zambia's sole export of any significance, plummeted on the world market, and the country incurred massive debts which, by the time MMD were elected in 1991, had reached more than US$7 billion, making Zambia the most indebted country in the world on a per capita basis.

A more insidious effect of public policy was, to undermine the strengths of traditional Zambian society and the ability of people to fend for themselves by encouraging a culture of state dependence. At the same time, the capacity of the state to provide for them was gradually whittled away.

## The New Economy

There was a heady excitement in Zambia as the restructuring process began in earnest in 1992. It was pure misfortune that the process began when the worst drought in living memory hit the country, but careful planning by the new administration mitigated the worst effects of the drought.

There has been a fair measure of success in implementing the structural reforms. By May, 1995, Zimco, the umbrella organisation sheltering the myriad parastatals, had been dismantled and a privatisation programme was underway, overseen by a new body called the Zambia Privatisation Agency. So run down were the parastatals that privatisation has been a slow process, not helped by the fact that departing managements had asset-stripped many of the businesses. As the President himself has wryly observed, "You cannot force people to buy what they are not interested in."

Banking was deregulated and currency controls removed with the Kwacha floating more or less freely, and import procedures were eased. Interest rates dropped and inflation, which had been running as high as 183 per cent, was sharply reduced.

Revenue collection was improved with the establishment of the Zambia Revenue Authority (ZRA) which has acted toughly to bring about compliance. However, some actions surrounding the new tax regime have given cause for concern. Zambia's productive base was made all but moribund by policies pursued during the Kaunda years, and investment in traditional areas such as agriculture, manufacturing and tourism is slow in coming, with few incentives for investors. Perhaps in response to the revenue shortfall produced by the lack of a healthy productive base, personal and company taxes are high. In particular, customs levies on imported raw materials and on imported goods are much higher, generally, than those elsewhere in the region. By the time sales or value-added taxes and company taxes have been applied, goods and services in Zambia are priced at unrealistically high levels. Zambia is a poor regional competitor as a result. The Dunlop tyre factory is one example among many of a business that found the cost of imported raw materials made its own tyres unviable in the deregulated environment; the only way it could stay in business was to import and sell Dunlop tyres manufactured in Zimbabwe, and close down its own production line.

Just as manufactured goods were forced into uncompetitiveness by taxes, so too have tourism products. High taxes across the board and poor services make Zambia a forbiddingly high-cost tourist destination for most, when compared with regional competitors such as Zimbabwe, South Africa, Botswana and Namibia. This means that even the best tourist operations are marginal, although highly appreciated by an exclusive clientele, who return again and again to some of the best natural resources in Africa.

There has been, in addition, growing concern that the formal commercial sector is bearing a disproportionate burden of increased taxes and tougher collection measures. Most commercial activity in Zambia is carried out by the informal sector which is not taxed. Those who are being hit by zealous ZRA investigators are those who, because they are licensed, registered businesses, have tax records and are easy to target.

There is continuing concern that spending decisions within government are adding to the tax burden. Overspending on defence is an example. The purchase of heavy-duty military equipment has to be paid for and donors will not finance this.

State security is another area of heavy spending. The Kaunda years saw the growth in Zambia of a huge, and hugely incompetent, state spying network which used literally thousands of citizens to spy on their fellows. The Chiluba administration has been slow to disband this destabilising structure; instead it has reportedly paid millions of dollars to Israel to train Zambia's secret service.

Of primary concern has been the fate of Zambia Consolidated Copper Mines, which supplies 90 per cent of the country's foreign exchange earnings. Since 1968 the state has had a controlling stake in this large and unwieldy body, and even in Kaunda's time it was recognised that some degree of privatisation was unavoidable.

The importance of this lies in the fact that Zambia is a mono-economy, with the result that reduced earnings from copper damage not just the state, but small, private enterprises as well, many of which have been driven to the wall by unpaid bills. Government, in fact, has become the country's largest debtor. Political as well as financial factors have been hampering progress. Any attempt to make the mines more efficient would result in putting thousands out of work. This has already occurred, with serious repercussions, elsewhere in the public sector. Furthermore, some loss-making mines would need to be closed, following the example of Kabwe Mine which was closed with a severe economic and social impact on the town and district. Further closures would meet with stiff opposition from the powerful Mine Workers' Union, which was President Chiluba's original power base.

Corruption is a major problem, and has been for many years. The MMD government has also been badly tainted by corruption and allegations of drug dealing. Chiluba has called for evidence of corruption on the part of his ministers and officials, but the call has not received much response, probably owing to the threat of retribution. Pressure from donors has brought about some change, and in particular is believed to have led to the resignation of two ministers who were reportedly involved in drug dealing. Pressure from donors contributed to the passing of the Ministerial Code of Conduct Act in 1994, which required ministers to disclose their personal assets and interests. One disclosed assets of more than US$6 million. In general, however, the existence of corruption or drug activity is detected only by the obvious signs of massive wealth held by some senior government officers and businessmen, wealth on a scale unlikely to be possible through normal salaries or business returns. Lack of hard evidence and the self-protecting nature of the government/business elite mean that prosecutions are few.

Although the process of structural reform is having some success, it is having a serious impact on Zambia's social structure. The donor community is sponsoring the reform process and insisting on adherence to it, and at the same time it is they who must intervene to help alleviate the worst effects of that reform. In that sense, and for the time being at least, Zambia's independence is compromised. The country simply does not have the money or skills to put its own house in order.

Tens of thousands of workers have been retrenched as a result of restructuring and this has brought enormous pressure on the ability of people to provide such basics as food, clothing and shelter for their families. Reductions in Government spending have led to the removal of subsidies on maize meal (the staple food), fuel, transport, fertilisers and so on, which have all increased in price as a result. In addition, the demand for a leaner national budget has resulted in a fee-paying regime in such areas as health and education.

Life expectancy is falling and infant mortality is increasing, as is illiteracy, with falling levels of school enrolments. Over half of Zambian households are below the poverty line, while some are "core poor", meaning that an adequate diet is beyond reach even if all their income is spent on food.

Radical health and education reforms are being addressed by the Government with backing from the international donor community, and are starting to show results. Other countries throughout Africa are watching Zambia's reform process with some interest since its central political premise is to decentralise and devolve decision-making to districts and grass root communities. Statistics suggest a long battle ahead to reverse the decline, but the process is now well underway.

In the meantime, Zambia remains a land of great natural beauty, much of it unknown to visitors and Zambians alike. Apart from the Victoria Falls, the country is blessed with lakes, rivers, forests and mountains of fantastic variety. Its people are renowned for their warmth and cheerfulness and their resilience in seeking to overcome the adversity that has befallen their young nation. Wildlife, too, is incredibly diverse. This, coupled with a rich cultural tradition, makes the country extremely attractive.

The photographs on the following pages are a glimpse of it.

# Urban Life

Zambia is one of the most urbanised countries on the African continent. 35 per cent of her people live in settlements with more than 20,000 inhabitants – three times the proportion in most African countries – and a great many Zambians show a strong liking for living in the cities.

The principal urban centres, Lusaka, Livingstone and the towns on the Copperbelt, are smaller and newer than their counterparts in Europe and America. They are also a good deal poorer: for the most part they lack the social amenities of the world's larger cities. Nonetheless, what Zambian towns lack in facilities they make up for in the variety, humour and liveliness of their people. Few European towns can match the profusion of colours of a Kamwala market on any day of the week. Women's dresses in yellows, greens, whites and blues hang in rows, rack upon rack, or are laid on the ground in vivid mosaics of primary colours. The fruit and vegetables on the market stalls are stacked in a way to attract the maximum attention from passers by.

Zambia's capital, Lusaka, is now home to one in ten of the country's population. It was started as a railway siding in 1905, but grew rapidly because it stood on the junction of rail routes from north and south, as well as roads leading to all four points of the compass. Originally the centre of a farming community, Lusaka became increasingly industrialised as the Copperbelt grew 200 kilometres up the railway line to the north. The town assumed capital status in 1935, and has since become the country's principal point of contact with the outside world, housing all the major government departments and foreign embassies. The commercial centre includes the head offices of international and major national undertakings, most of which are now housed in multi-storey buildings.

Outside Lusaka, most of the big towns are found on the Copperbelt. Kitwe, Ndola, Mufulira and Chingola are the largest of these, but although they owe their existence primarily to copper, many secondary industries have now grown up. Earthenware pipemaking, clothing manufacture, joinery and food processing are all big employers.

The main tourist centre for Zambia is Livingstone, situated close to the Victoria Falls on the border with Zimbabwe. Near the town, a small game park enables visitors to the Falls to see something of Zambia's wildlife. Livingstone is also the home of a museum, which houses a large collection of historical and metallurgical exhibits, including relics of David Livingstone himself. Livingstone was the capital of Zambia (then Northern Rhodesia) before Lusaka.

Like much of Africa, Zambia is suffering a massive urban influx from the countryside. Younger people in particular are lured by the prospect of jobs, but are frequently disappointed. The result has been a ring of shanty towns around Lusaka and the other larger cities, where unemployment is high and violence is never far beneath the surface. In most cases, housing is sub-standard while sanitation and water supply are often pitifully inadequate. Children in the shanties are frequently malnourished and vulnerable to infection. Both violent crime and black marketeering are endemic.

But the shanties are filled with a people who have made a fine art out of surviving from very slender means. In Europe, as soon as a shoe is damaged or down at heel, it is quickly consigned to the rubbish bin. In a Zambian town, by the bus stop or under the shade of a tree or in the market place, there are men who sit surrounded by heaps of broken shoes, patiently cobbling them back to life. Along Freedom Way in Lusaka, tailors can stitch repairs for you while you wait.

Nonetheless, politicians expend a great deal of energy in trying to persuade rural dwellers to stay in the countryside. They have introduced 'reconstruction centres' aimed at resettling young people and providing them with all the necessities of agricultural production. Although the youths in these centres are initially given free board and lodging, there is a high rate of defection. For in spite of the dirt and discomfort of the city, its allure is powerful. The countryside may be healthier, more open and free, but to many of the rural young, it is cramped and monotonous. Compared with the profligate variety of town life, the village offers little other than the means to earn a living. A town on the Copperbelt plays fast and loose with both nerves and money; but the attractions which they present sharpen one's sense of what it is to be a town-dweller.

The result is a demographic pattern characteristic in most African cities: most of the migrant population are under 25 years of age. They are predominantly men, since the womenfolk of the villages are tied down by responsibilities for their families and household property. Until recently, men would often come into the cities on a temporary basis in order to supply wages for relatives in the countryside. But increasingly, the traditional extended family obligations are being supplanted by a need to cater for one's immediate relatives. The result has been an acceleration of the move to the cities, since fewer rural dwellers are being supported by wage earners in urban employment.

But there is another class of citizen, a world removed from the shanty towns in which the poorer people live. Lusaka in particular is home to a large proportion of *abakankala*, government officials and bureaucrats who live in the low density suburbs which used to be inhabited by colonial administrators. These people do not constitute the bulk of Zambia's city dwellers, youths at the other end of the income scale who often have no means of support at all.

As Zambia moves toward the 21st century, she finds herself in the unenviable position of leading the way in what is now a pan-African trend. If it continues, a continent of farmers and hunters will, in a generation's time, have become a continent of city dwellers. Even today, Zambia faces a two sided task. One is to persist in her efforts to lure the urban young back to the villages. The other is to ensure that those who simply won't budge from the cities are gainfully employed. The task is not an easy one - and the nation will have a high price to pay if she fails.

Lusaka grew outward from its railway line, and Cairo Road *(bottom)*, that runs parallel to it, has the largest concentration of high rise buildings.

The Lusaka Stock Exchange *(right)* is a visible manifestation of the newly liberalised economy.

The Meridian Building *(above)* is an outstanding example of appropriate architecture for Africa, not only in its stylised village-complex design, but also in its use of local materials.

Looking north along Cha Cha Cha Road *(left)* the evolution of Lusaka's architecture from house plots to high rise offices is evident.

It is not unusual to find Zambian women occupying the highest positions in politics, commerce and the professions. Their success in these areas marks a break with tradition on much of the African continent, where they have been servile throughout recorded history.

Current wisdom is that giving alms to beggars only perpetuates this way of living. There is a growing effort to provide alternatives to street begging by means of community-based projects.

In Lusaka the crime level, especially theft, has been high and the inability of the police to contain it has led to a consequent surge in the private security business.

The HIV/AIDS epidemic is regarded by many as the biggest single problem facing Zambia. Anti-AIDS activities are now almost a way of life with the message being spread in street paintings, street theatre, and radio.

(*Above right*) Shops built about the time the capital was transferred from Livingstone to Lusaka in 1935.

(*Below right*) From late October to April, Lusaka is often drenched with torrential rain.

25

Small minibuses *(left)* are the staple form of transport for literally millions of Africans. They often function as a meeting place for the exchange of the latest gossip. They are quick - some-times too quick in the opinion of some motorists - and economical.

The international airport at Lusaka *(below left)* has recently undergone a refurbishment programme. Able to cope with the largest of intercontinental jets, the runway has been better maintained than others in Africa which handle a far higher volume of traffic.

The railway *(below right)* from Lusaka to the Copperbelt has traditionally been a major communications artery in the country, but branch lines to other provincial outreaches continue to make Zambia heavily dependent on rail transport.

(*Previous page*) The University of Zambia opened in 1966 with 312 students. Today its enrolment exceeds 4,000, with campuses at Lusaka, Kitwe, and Ndola. At Independence in 1964, Zambia had under 100 university graduates and under 1000 men and women with full secondary education. Not surprisingly, free universal education was high on the Government's priorities - and women benefitted as much as men.

(*Below left and opposite*) At the University of Zambia, many of the women follow courses in the Humanities and Social Sciences.

Founded in 1963 with an enrolment of 33, Lusaka's International School now has in the region of a thousand students from many different language backgrounds.

*Opposite* It is six thirty in the morning, but already this woman has been up for two hours. By dusk at five thirty, she hopes to be rid of her heavy consignment of tomatoes, which will disappear in dribs and drabs throughout the day. When they reach the dinner table, the tomatoes will still be young, sweet and fresh. Their vendor will be an old woman by the time she is forty five.

Most of those engaged in small business *(top)* do so unhampered by the newfound rigours of the tax authorities. However, the formal sector of the economy is suffering badly from the zealous pursuit of taxes which now dampen the ardour of entrepreneurs.

The maintenance of vehicles *(middle)* is an uphill struggle in Zambia. Few mechanics or dealers in spares have much by the way of formal training, and the culture of precision necessary for the maintenance of a high technology economy is largely absent.

Thirty years ago, the sewing of women's clothes *(bottom)* would have been unthinkable for the average Zambian male: a life extracting copper from the earth would have been considered far more appropriate. But the world is changing, and the state can no longer be guaranteed to keep miners in wages for life. Consequently, Zambia is witnessing a diversification of male activities, of which this is but one.

The discovery of copper in the north of the country has led to major urbanisation outside the capital. Chingola, Chililabombwe, Mufulira, Ndola and Kitwe are all large cities by African standards.

Migration from the countryside poses an acute problem to the Zambian government: as the population explodes in the urban areas, the coutryside is losing its young people. They leave in search of a job in town, but when they get there, there is often no employment to be had. A large ring of slums provides a ragged edge to most of the smart city centres.

*(Left)* In Zambia, music and dance are inextricably linked. Dancing can be just for fun, but more often it is connected with the rituals of good health, prosperity and security, or with the cycle of birth, marriage and death. Most dances involve group participation but occasionally, soloists get the chance to display their virtuoso technique. During this century, Zambian traditional culture has been affected by foreign influences. As radio and television sets proliferate, music and dance reflect the sights and sounds of foreign cultures.

(Below) Most of Zambia's Asian minority comes from a narrow strip of the Gujarat Province of Western India. They came mainly into the retail trade in the first decades of the century, but their children and grandchildren have moved into manufacturing and the professions. With the British expatriate community now diminished, it is the Asians who are largely responsible for keeping cricket alive. Most towns in Zambia have their Hindu temples.

*(Previous page and below)* Soccer is Zambia's national game and a matter for serious discussion in bars and conference rooms alike. It is played at every level, from the international stadium to the dusty village pitch. The Zambian National Team has gained international recognition and several players have been transferred to major teams in Europe.

# Mining

Copper has been extracted in central Africa for several thousand years. Until this century, only surface deposits were exploited, but technological advances in the 1920s allowed access to the much richer bodies which lay hidden beneath a thick layer of topsoil.

Today, Zambia produces over half a million tonnes of copper every year, making her the fifth largest producer in the world. She also mines cobalt, ranking second in world production, as well as smaller quantities of other minerals. Although Zambia's copper reserves are beginning to run out, the mining industry is still the largest contributor to national income. It is also the largest pool of labour skills. Copper employs Zambians in over 3,000 different job categories, engineers, metallurgists, nurses, accountants and computer experts among them.

Virtually all this activity takes place in the famous Copperbelt, in the north of the country. It is an area 50 kilometres by 110 kilometres, and represents the biggest industrial concentration in Black Africa.

The ancient Africans used copper both for functional and decorative purposes. They mined the richest malachite ores either from trenches or from circular shafts, usually ten to fifteen metres deep. Furnaces were built from anthill material and fuelled with charcoal. In Africa, as elsewhere in ancient times, the ceremony of smelting had strong religious and magical importance, with the Spirits of the Mountain showing their power by the miracle of melting stones to produce metal.

The first white prospectors came in 1895, two Americans charged by Cecil Rhodes with finding a railway route to the north - and minerals to pay for it. Neither they nor others who followed had much luck. The first big discoveries came in the Shaba region of what is now Zaire. There, copper deposits occupied the crests of hills rising 50 to 100 metres above the surrounding country. Their metal content made them bare of trees, and the green oxides in the outcrops gave brilliant visual displays which left no doubt about the presence of copper.

Zambia had much longer to wait. Where movement of the earth's crust had thrust the Shaba deposits upwards, those only a few miles away in Zambia had been pushed down. They were covered by a thick layer of soil, and were of a grade too low to be considered valuable. For the Copperbelt, the starting point was in 1902, when a prospector, William Collier, shot a roan antelope at the request of an African who said he was too old to hunt. It fell on copper stained rock in a clearing on the banks of the Luanshya stream. Next morning he shot a reedbuck in another clearing, near another outcrop. Collier investigated and found he had walked along a giant hairpin with arms two kilometres long. To his practised eye, the absence of vegetation indicated the presence of copper.

The value of his discovery had to wait nearly a quarter of a century to be exploited. At Kansanshi and Bwana Mkubwa there were bursts of mining activity, but the real treasure lay buried until after the First World War, when demand for copper began to rise dramatically. The richest ores which responded to treatment by heat alone were running out.

Fortunately at around the same time, the problem of extracting small quantities of valuable mineral from large amounts of barren rock was solved by the development of flotation. By grinding the ore into a fine powder and stirring it up in a suitable fluid, the mineral particles could now be attached to air bubbles while the useless grains of rock sank to the bottom of the container. By this method, mineral content of a very few parts in a hundred could be profitably mined.

The British South Africa Company now governed the country and owned its mineral rights. They decided that since little or nothing had developed from small companies and lone prospectors, exclusive prospecting rights over large areas should be given to wealthy companies with the financial capital to invest in expensive plant.

By the end of 1925, it was becoming clear that the poor quality oxides on the surface were just the weathered tips of huge, easily treated sulphides lying at a greater depth. In 1926, theory gave way to certainty. A bold drilling programme was carried out where William Collier had been hunting a quarter of a century earlier. The drill brought up material from 160 metres containing nearly four per cent copper. One of the world's great mining industries was born.

It nearly collapsed as soon as it started. In the 1930s the Depression bit hard, and the price of copper on the world markets fell catastrophically. But the industry struggled on until it was saved by the prospect of a second global war in the late 1930s, for new weapons with copper components were now needed in large numbers.

The demands of war accelerated development, and in 1943, Copperbelt production reached a quarter of a million tonnes each year. Its final salvation came in 1949, when the devaluation of sterling ensured the industry's prosperity. Chibuluma and Konkola mines were developed, Chambishi came back to life, Mufulira was expanded, and Nchanga grew into one of the world's biggest and richest mines. In 1969, the Copperbelt produced three quarters of a million tonnes, its highest figure ever.

But this was a year marked by an even more significant event in the industry's history - nationalisation. One of the priorities of Zambia's leadership after the creation of the new state five years earlier had been to establish national control over natural resources. Before Independence, the mines had been owned by companies and shareholders overseas, and even the right to mine was outside the government's control. Negotiations between Britain, Zambia and the British South Africa Company continued until the very eve of Independence on 23rd October 1964, before the Company finally relinquished control.

Today, copper is not the highly valued commodity that it once was. It still plays a valuable role in the electrical industry because of its high conductivity, and it is also widely used in transport and engineering. But fibre optics and the silicon chip have played a large part in reducing copper's value on the world market in real terms the price of copper has halved since Independence.

Consequently the mining industry has had to draw up long term plans to deal with the inevitable day when the Copperbelt ceases to mine. The industry is now investing capital and labour into agricultural developments and small-scale industries which can absorb future redundancies. No-one doubts that it will be a long and difficult task to replace the comparative ease of metal extraction and export. But the battle has begun.

*(Far left and previous page)* Just as huge earthmovers and giant trucks transformed the economy of opencast operations, so did the compressed air drill revolutionise underground mining and tunnelling.

*(Below)* Copperbelt miners await the train which will carry them to the workface, now, after 50 years of mining, many hundreds of metres from the shaft.

Before the final casting *(above)*, copper is
passed through converters *(right)* where
air is blown into cylindrical furnaces,
a process which removes the iron and
sulphur impurities. Each of the
furnaces at the Nkana Refinery holds 200
tonnes of molten metal.

(*Left*) At Kitwe, molten slag is tipped on heaps which have been growing for more than half a century. Passers-by on the approach road are given a spectacular display at night.

(*Below*) Finished cobalt ready for export.

The horizontal bed filters at TLP3. The third stage of the tailings leach plant at Nchanga can process up to 3m tonnes a month of previously treated material to recover valuable solutions from unwanted solids.

A maze of pipes illustrates the complexity of the roast-leach-electrowin plant at Nkana, which uses chemical, thermal and electrolytic processes to reclaim cobalt.

*Opposite* The Swarp Spinning mills in Ndola is a Zambian success story. It employs nearly a thousand workers and produces over 6,500 metric tons of yarn a year, 95 per cent of which is exported to Europe.

The privatisation of companies that used to belong to the Industrial Development Corporation has improved productivity and management.

# Agriculture

**A**lmost one tenth of Zambia's arable land is at present agriculturally utilized and seventy per cent of the working population are engaged in some sort of farming. Since agriculture is the only major alternative to copper as a foreign exchange earner, Zambia needs to export sufficient cash crops to replace the income lost by the copper industry's decline.

In the colonial days, the large-scale commercial farmers were mainly Europeans. They made a substantial contribution to crop production, but many decided not to continue after Independence. The bulk of the rural population contributed little to this production, and constituted no viable market for the products of other sectors of the economy. Thus, in the mid-1960s, an ambitious programme of crop production was embarked upon.

Only a succession of droughts in recent years has prevented Zambia from meeting all her needs in maize, the staple diet. In order to reduce import bills, steps have been taken to produce seed potatoes locally, while commercial storage of Zambian-grown onions has largely offset out-of-season shortages. Increasing urbanisation is leading to a change in dietary habits, with an ever-growing demand for wheat products in place of maize meal. This is an important challenge to the government, since 30 per cent of wheat is imported, using up valuable foreign exchange.

Zambian agriculture is characterised by a sharp contrast between large commercial concerns on one hand and thousands of small subsistence farms on the other. In the villages, most of the agricultural work is done by women, while the men tend to stay at home. There are over half a million subsistence farms in Zambia, but hardly any of them are mechanised and the use of animal draught power is only just developing. Only one per cent of the agricultural land in Zambia is irrigated, which leaves food production vulnerable to drought. Farmers are now being encouraged by the government to concentrate on the cultivation of sorghum and millet, which can survive more easily in dry areas than maize.

Cattle are very numerous in Zambia, but 90 per cent of them are owned by traditional herders. Important as status symbols and sources of wealth, they are not killed for meat and are rarely sold. Their main practical uses are for dairy products and as a source of manure. Cattle are the principle source of wealth for many people in Southern, Central and Eastern Provinces, but their numbers are so great that they are causing environmental problems. Overgrazing has resulted in soil erosion, while selective grazing of the more productive grass species has encouraged the spread of coarser ones.

This situation is partly a legacy of the colonial era: before Independence, Africans and their livestock were confined to 'trust lands', reserves which usully had poor soils. As a result, the density of the livestock increased, which led to overgrazing damage. Goats, too, have been invaluable for many subsistence farmers, but in some areas they have been allowed to eat almost everything, turning the land into a collection of dust bowls.

The erosion of fertile soils presents Zambia with one of her most pressing challenges. Soils take hundreds or even thousands of years to form, but can be destroyed in a matter of hours and Zambia's cultivated lands probably lose around three million tonnes of topsoil every year. Erosion of the soil is caused by deforestation, over-grazing, and inept agricultural practices. All these activities remove vegetation cover and expose the soil to wind and rain. In heavy storms, soil is washed away and, as run-off water gains momentum, large gullies are formed. The eroded soils rob farmers of their livelihood, and build up in rivers and reservoirs, causing floods as a result.

Before Independence, considerable energy was invested in preventing soil erosion. Most of the cultivated fields were contoured, while storm drains, windbreaks, and terraces were common. There are still many areas where the land continues to be well protected with small fields, contour ridging and strip cropping, but since colonial days the economy has become more cash-orientated, and farmers are responding more to the activities which produce direct economic benefits. Soil conservation works have fallen into disrepair and farmers receive little advice on the preservation of their lifeblood.

Although arable agriculture has suffered as a result of soil erosion, this has been offset to some extent by the use of pesticides. They are the main weapons against crop losses, which used to run at 30 per cent. Cotton would be virtually impossible to produce without pesticides, and yields of other crops would be much lower. Zambia clearly gains a great deal from these chemicals, but their application is largely uncontrolled. Containers are rarely labelled to warn of their dangerous contents, and workers applying the chemicals frequently do not wear protective clothing. Because safety standards are known to be lax, certain chemical companies 'dump' pesticides on Zambia, selling chemicals which are either old or banned elsewhere.

In spite of these difficulties, the Zambian government is keenly aware of the need to make agriculture a big cash earner for the future. One of the most exciting possibilities is the development of rice as a major crop. By African standards, Zambia has an abundance of water resources, particularly around the Bangweulu swamps and along the Zambezi flood plain. Production of rice has been increasing in recent years, but its potential has hardly been explored. It has an advantage over maize in that it can grow in areas less vulnerable to drought and could, if incorporated into the domestic diet, go a long way towards reducing Zambia's dependence on imported wheat. As in all areas of Zambia's economic life, self-reliance and diversity are the two keys to future prosperity. This is particularly true of agriculture - for in the medium term, there is no other substitute for copper on the horizon.

# Commercial Farming

Zambian yields of maize are as good as any in the world, and though mechanisation is a feature of large commercial farms, small-scale farmers using draught animals and manual labour get results just as good. With the high foreign exchange cost of imported machinery, government policy is to boost small scale production.

A sugar refinery was opened at Ndola in 1960, but it depended on imported raw sugar. In 1968, the Zambia Sugar Company was formed by Indeco in partnership with Tate & Lyle, and the development of the Nakambala Estate in the Southern Province began. Now Nakambala has 10,000 hectares under cane, and there are two refineries capable of refining over 150,000 tonnes of sugar a year. Products have diversified to include jams, syrup, treacle and molasses. Zambia became self-sufficient in sugar in 1975 and is now developing export markets.

At Nakambala, over a million tonnes of cane are grown under irrigation each year.

*(Previous page)* Before harvesting, the crop is fired to burn off the leaves.

*(These pages)* An army of seasonal workers is employed to cut the cane. A successful small growers scheme adjacent to the Nakambala estate has opened opportunities for Zambian small scale farmers to become commercial cane growers in their own right.

*(Left)* The growing urban population likes white bread, so to cut the drain on foreign reserves caused by wheat imports, great efforts are being made to grow the crop locally. One example is the EEC-funded Mpongwe wheat and soya scheme, but this type of project requires immense capital investment and intensive management.

Tea is the country's newest commercial crop, and is grown under irrigation in the Luapula Province. The first plantation was established as a government — owned project, the Kawambwa Tea Company Limited, in the 1970's, and is now producing much of Zambia's needs. Local people are being encouraged to grow their own on a small scale alongside the estate.

## Subsistence Farming

In spite of the importance of commercial agriculture, most of the Zambia's farmers operate on small subsistence holdings. There are more than 600,000 of them altogether, scattered across the nation.

The traditional drought resistant crops of millet and sorghum were largely replaced by maize, which was introduced by the Portugese in the 16th century. Now that bread has become popular with urban consumers the demand for wheat has grown. However, maize remains the stable diet in the rural areas.

Livestock is also overwhelmingly in the hands of traditional herders. Cattle are rarely killed for beef, but constitute a source of milk and manure for crops. Because buffalo have not been domesticated with any success in Zambia (as they have in India), cattle are also used for haulage in the countryside. Grazing of cattle and goats takes place on a free-range basis, is frequently uncontrolled, and causes a great deal of soil erosion as a result.

There is clearly much that can be done to make subsistence farming more efficient in the future, and the Government has launched a nationwide agricultural programme aimed particularly at subsistence cultivators.

# Fishing

Thanks to the abundance of lakes and rivers in Zambia, many rural people depend far more on fish than on meat for their food.

*(Right)* Lake Bangwuelu, although shallow, is one of the largest in Africa, and is surrounded by vast expanses of swamp, forming a reservoir for the Luapula and Congo Rivers.

Fishing takes many forms,
from large scale commercial
netting to the small boy with
his hook and line.
The traditional ways of catch-
ing are as varied as the fish
themselves......

80

........barriers across rivers, woven baskets, traps of a dozen kinds, nets, barbed spears and harpoons - even bows and arrows have been used to catch fish in Zambia. Every ethnic group has its own speciality.

As early as 1860, the explorer Richard Burton
described the use of circular nets lowered from
a canoe to catch fish attracted by the light of the
wood-fired brazier.

The kapenta fishermen of Lake Kariba still bring in
their catch of African whitebait in immense round
dip nets. Nowadays the fish are dried in the sun and  shipped
by road in quantity to the towns and cities.

# Rural Life

**B**efore Europeans arrived, Africa's economy was essentially a rural one. Agriculture, fishing and hunting were the means whereby each family supported itself, and in southern Africa where the population density was very low, these activities were viable.

Now, for better or worse, the city is a powerful magnet to the young and rural population is rapidly declining. It is mainly men who leave their villages to find jobs, either in the Copperbelt or along the railway line. Behind them, they leave young wives who settle in their husbands' villages and have to depend on subsistence farming, fishing and whatever financial assistance the men can send back.

In recent years there has been a trend by retired public servants to return to their home villages and engage in some farming. Such people also provide occasional jobs in their communities. However, virtually all available part-time work is for men, so that the women, who are far greater in number, have to depend on their own ingenuity to raise cash. The most popular and profitable occupation is beer brewing. In order to improve sales, care is usually taken to ensure that not too many people in one village have beer for sale on the same day.

In appearance, Zambian rural villages look similar to those in the rest of Africa. The cheapest and most common type of rural abode is made of sticks, and plastered with clayey earth which is often mixed with cow-dung. The actual construction and thatching of houses is done by men, while women plaster the walls and prepare the floor, using the same materials. Houses made of burnt bricks and concrete blocks are also built, but they usually belong to local officials or businessmen who can afford them. Many of the amenities taken for granted in the towns simply do not exist here, and work can be hard for meagre returns.

Adulthood comes early to rural children. They are required to help look after younger siblings or any other children in the village, for villages are usually composed of people who are all related to one another. They also learn how to cook and carry out other household duties much earlier than town children. Girls in particular assume their adult duties at a young age. Few manage to start school before they are ten years old, but after just five years of primary education, a girl is considered to be an adult at the age of 15.

At this age, she quickly takes on grown-up responsibilities, including marriage, child rearing and harvesting of the crops. All this happens while her urban counterpart is still considered a child in secondary school. Only a small percentage of rural children ever complete the seven years of formal learning which constitutes primary education. This is due mainly to the cost of school uniforms, books and various school funds to which parents must contribute, all of which place a great burden on rural families. Very few children from the countryside make it to university.

Despite the lack of opportunities, there is an enviable side to rural life in Zambia. Nobody has to face a problem alone: joys and sorrows are shared alike. Women are scarcely seen alone gathering firewood or fishing. Fetching water, collecting mushrooms, or doing laundry at the stream are chores which are often turned into enjoyable social events. When there is a funeral or wedding to be organised everybody contributes otherwise the whole exercise would be too costly for those directly concerned.

Weddings, initiation ceremonies, healing sessions and beer parties provide leisure and entertainment for rural communities. These are usually held at weekends when people are not expected to work in the fields. Initiation ceremonies usually last two days and a night, while weddings can last even longer, depending on the affluence of the families concerned. Food and drink for such occasions are provided by members of the family and well-wishers. No formal invitation is ever made to any of these activities, and even passers-by are welcome to join in.

When a bride comes to her husband's village, she expects to live in a house of her own, using utensils provided by her husband. It is unacceptable that a wife should live with her in-laws, no matter how temporary the arrangement. This means that before a man can think of getting a wife, he should build himself a house if he does not already have one.

Healing sessions start in the late afternoon or early evening and go on until morning, after which there is a great deal of beer drinking for the rest of the day. The so-called 'witch-doctor' is really something of a spiritual healer-cum-herbalist, in whom village communities place more faith than their urban counterparts have in the medical practitioner.

Although western-style clinics and health centres are scattered throughout the rural areas, many villagers would rather pay astronomical fees to traditional healers than go for free medical treatment. Taking a patient to a healer can often cost as much as a cow or the cash equivalent. This happens whether or not the patient is cured, and people do not seem to think this exorbitant. It is a testament to the charisma of traditional healers that they are still able to hold such sway in village life, despite the obvious benefits in health care which Government centres and missionary clinics have brought to the countryside.

Like most other states in Africa, Zambia is committed to a programme of 'rural development', for the Government appreciates the importance which agriculture is going to play in the future of the country. There is also a clear understanding of the need to maintain some of the traditional life which existed before Zambia became a modern, cosmopolitan state. Consequently the Government invests keenly in rural schools, health centres and agricultural extension schemes. If mineral reserves become depleted in the coming decades, it will be essential to have a well-planned infrastructure already in place to provide employment opportunities outside the Copperbelt. The key to Zambia's future success lies largely in the natural and human resources which her own countryside can offer.

A traditional Zambian village comprises thirty or forty huts near fields of maize or millet, for which the women are responsible. The surrounding forest too is their preserve, where wild vegetables, mushrooms and honey are gathered. The men hunt where there is game to be found. The white ant poses a major threat to the structural integrity of mud buildings: whole villages move every few years and new ground must be cultivated. Poor material living standards are offset by a strong sense of community, for the obligations of the extended family ensure a system of communal support. In particular, the elderly are still very closely involved in the running of village life, in contrast to their counterparts in the west, who are seen increaseingly as a burden.

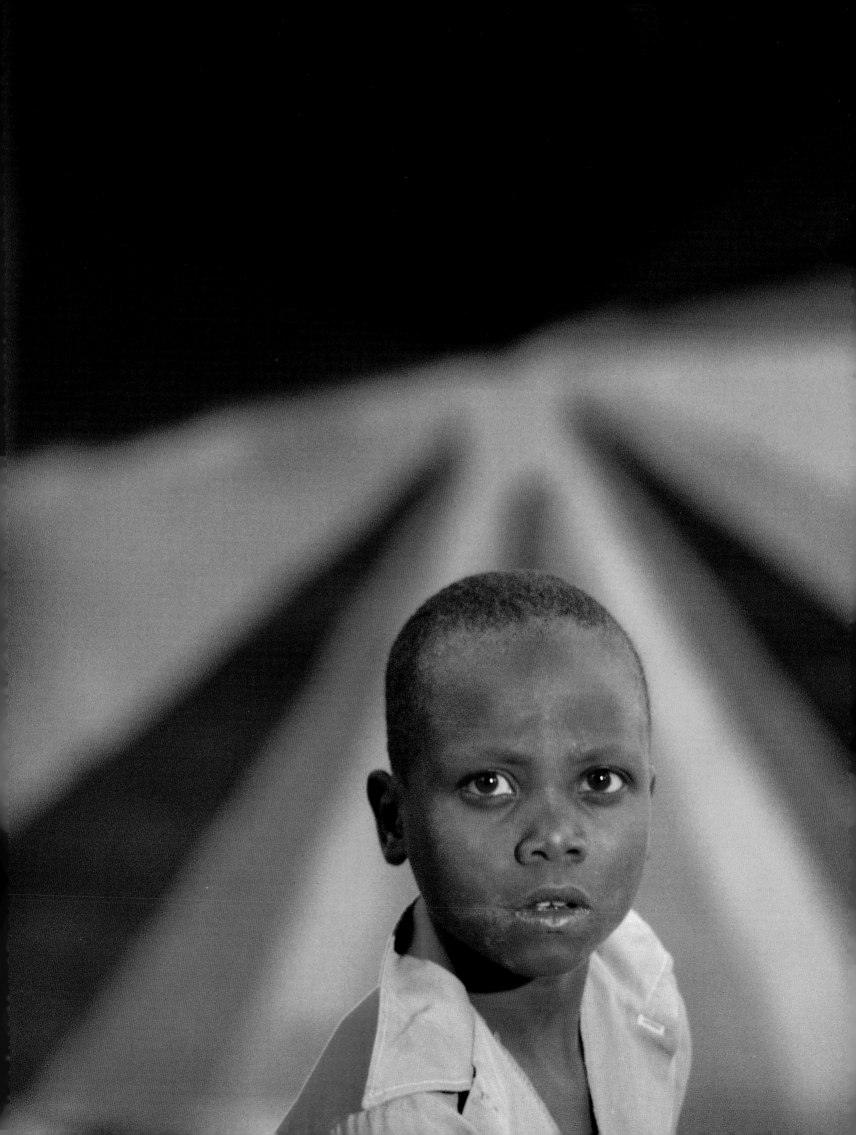

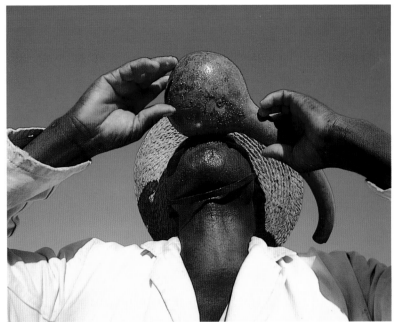

A life of labour starts early for rural women, and
motherhood can begin at fifteen. The basic diet of maize
or cassava is usually varied with vegetables,
such as beans *(left)* and bulrush millet *(above)*.

Country life in Zambia is changing rapidly with the advent of the cash economy. The calabash is being replaced by the galvanised bucket and the cigarette is displacing the hand-made pipe.

The villages are peopled mainly by women, children and the elderly: there is often a striking absence of able bodied men.

*(This page, clockwise from right)* A Southern Province boy tests his swing made of plaited grass. On his head, he carries a catapult made from strips of inner tube. He uses it for shooting birds.

A woman's daily task, carrying water from stream or well to the family quarters, often involves a journey of several hours.

A Northern Province village near the fishing port of Mpulungu is close enough to urban life to be beset by city styles and transport on wheels. With no electricity, the young man keeps his trousers pressed with a charcoal iron.

This village woman supports her family by cultivating the fields, but her daughter may work at a computer terminal in an air conditioned room.

*(Opposite page)* In the absence of running water, laundry is still washed in pools, but villagers must beware the crocodiles which claim hundreds of lives each year.

*(Following page)* Children already form half the population of Zambia, and the imbalance between young and old will increase dramatically in the coming years.

# Natural Resources

The next quarter century is likely to be a transition period for Zambia. Since the 1930s the country has depended heavily on one commodity for her economic well-being: copper. There will come a time soon when all the economic deposits have been worked out, and the country will have to fall back on other resources - agriculture, forestry and tourism - in order to survive in the 21st century. At the same time, conservation of the environment will remain of paramount importance,

and the balance between these priorities is likely to be a major preoccupation for the country's leaders.

Unlike some of her neighbours, Zambia is well endowed with natural resources. Apart from copper, the country also has workable deposits of cobalt, lead, zinc, and tin. There is water in abundance, not just for domestic use, but to drive hydro-electric turbines. While there is not much first-rate soil for agriculture, there are huge areas of valuable woodland. Zambia is also blessed with a variety of wildlife sufficient to attract tourists from all over the world. It is the conservation of these resources, without hindering the country's economic growth, which is perhaps Zambia's main challenge for the future.

Most of the country's land lies under forest. Miombo woodland - an open mixture of shrubs, trees and tall grasses - covers about 70 per cent of the country. This vast resource is capable of providing a wide range of benefits for the people of Zambia. Timber provides construction material for houses and other buildings, the railway lines run on wooden sleepers and the Copperbelt mines are literally supported by wooden props. Wood is also essential for cooking and heating in nine out of every ten Zambian homes. Whole forests provide protection for the soil by protecting it from the drying effect of the sun and breaking the destructive forces of heavy rain. They also ensure a reliable water supply by acting as vast 'sponges' which hold water and release it gradually.

While most of the country's natural woodland is not under immediate threat, the indiscriminate cutting of trees around many of the towns is a major cause for concern. Zambia loses half a per cent of her woodlands each year, and around the cities this proportion is much higher. The main reason for the deforestation is that trees are such an important source of domestic fuel. Lately, more land has also been cleared for large scale agriculture, and forests are being cut illegally for construction without young trees being left for regeneration. If allowed to continue unchecked, the consequences for Zambia could be disastrous. Large areas of land would turn to desert, there would be serious landslides and floods, dams would be blocked by sedimentation, wildlife would suffer, and there would be a serious shortage of forest products. Reforestation is currently needed to counter the threat. In particular, fuelwood plantations are needed to meet the growing domestic demand.

Woodland aside, wildlife is another precious resource, both in maintaining the balance of nature and attracting foreign tourists. The country is home to over 100 mammals, including lion, hippo, leopard, elephant and buffalo. There are several species which can be found nowhere else in the world. More than 700 different birds are found in the country altogether, including the fish eagle, which has been adopted as Zambia's national emblem. The appeal of Zambia's wildlife is enhanced by the fact that the country is not yet overrun by tourists. In the national parks, the visitor can still experience a genuine sense of wilderness.

There are eighteen separate National Parks in Zambia. Altogether they cover nearly 60,000 square kilometres - about the size of Holland and Belgium combined. Most of them are chiefly intended for the preservation of mammals, but the parks are also designed to conserve unique systems of vegetation.

The biggest threat to Zambia's natural heritage comes from poachers. Even the national parks are not immune from them. There used to be far more elephants than there are now, but their numbers have been devastated by ivory-poaching gangs. They have been laid low by automatic rifles at the hands of men who care nothing for the wisdom, dignity and beauty of those they destroy. The black rhinoceros, once so common along the Luangwa River has almost disappered.

Wildlife Wardens patrol tens of thousands of square kilometres on foot, armed only with hunting rifles which cannot by law be fired except in self-defence. When they encounter a gang, there may only be five scouts trying to arrest as many as thirty poachers, armed with sophisticated automatic weapons. Far more by way of resources and training are needed if Zambia is not going to lose all of her elephants and rhino within the next generation.

Conservation is by no means an idea which is entirely new to Zambia. But until recently there has been no nationally co-ordinated management plan to make the most of its resources. While some natural assets are being destroyed or impaired, others have not been utilized to their full potential. The crucial factor behind successful policy will be balance: that policy will have failed if the country gains cheap electricity at the price of dried-up waterfalls, or short-term financial gain from uncontrolled tourism at the cost of the very sites the tourists have come to see.

It is in this context that the National Conservation Strategy for Zambia (NCSZ) has been formulated. The result of an intensive programme of consultations, it was prepared by the Ministry of Lands and Natural Resources. It stems from a document known as the World Conservation Strategy, which is based on the views of more than 700 scientists and 450 government agencies from over a hundred countries. To ensure that the objectives of conservation are achieved, the WCS recommends that every country reviews the progress within its own borders. The review is expected to form the basis of a national strategy. When it was officially adopted by the Party and its Government in July 1985, the NCS for Zambia became the first such strategy to be completed in Africa.

Every government should have the care of the environment high on its agenda. But it is easy to regard the long term trends of many environmental problems as too remote to justify immediate attention. Having recognised these problems and acknowledged that action needs to be taken, the task for Zambia now is to implement the National Conservation Strategy. The work has already begun.

The elephants were once monarchs of the Zambian bush. Today, they carry their tusks as a curse - the vast herds which roamed the woodlands have been massacred by poachers for the riches their ivory can bring. Gone forever are the big tuskers, the old bulls who followed their ancient trails: even the population of smaller elephants has been dramatically reduced by automatic rifles.

Of the many rivers which rise in the highlands of Zambia, the Luangwa is the most fascinating. It lacks the beauty of the Zambezi or the Kafue, yet possesses a grandeur enhanced by its wildlife, and evokes a spirit of old Africa which is fading fast away. From its humble beginnings in the Mafinga Mountains in North Eastern Zambia, the Luangwa flows southward for 700 kilometres to its convergence with the Zambezi. For most of this journey, it is a game haunted river: along its banks lives an abundance of elephant, buffalo, hippo, lion, leopard and giraffe. Several species in the Luangwa cannot be found anywhere else in the world. Placid and slow during the dry winter months, it becomes a raging torrent with the summer rains. The river's surging currents undercut its banks and sweep away trees that have stood for decades. Constantly changing and modifying its course with each successive rainy season, it cuts new channels to isolate the old, which become ox-bow lakes or lagoons. In the dry months these lagoons become a focal point for animals of every type which come to drink and graze on their silted shores. Herds of puku, the russet coated antelope, mingle with impala, zebra and waterbuck. As night falls, the grazing lawns become a magnet for the many hippo that have lain sleepily in the river shallows during the day. In the opposite direction come elephants to slake their thirst after a day in the forest. Extending back from the river on rising ground is a mosaic of different habitats. These contain hartebeest, roan and reed buck, as well as small numbers of sable antelope. All these species and many more comprise a richly diverse fauna which makes the Luangwa one of the finest wildlife areas of the world. At the centre of it all, is the murky meandering Luangwa, to whose banks the teaming herds come and go according to the seasons.

Wildlife Wardens and their scouts face an uphill struggle against the poachers. Armed only with hunting rifles, which cannot be fired except in self-defence, they have to tackle determined gangs of professional poachers armed with a range of sophisticated automatic weapons. Many poachers use Kalashnikov AK47s which were left over from the days when Zambia hosted the guerillas in the Rhodesian civil war.

There are 24 varieties of antelope recorded in Zambia, from the rare and tiny blue duiker to the huge eland. Here are a male kudu (far left), a bushbuck (left), and puku (below and bottom).

(previous page) Lechwe on the Kafue flats.

Lion are commonly seen in both the Kafue and Luangwa National Parks, often in groups twenty strong. They kill hartebeest, warthog, antelope, hippo, zebra and buffalo.

Visitors from all over the world come to the Luangwa Valley National Park because of the close contact it offers with animals in their natural habitat. Unlike many other parks in Africa, it is possible to drive through the Luangwa for a whole day without encountering another vehicle.

Buffalo find safety in numbers, but when a herd breaks into a stampede, natural enemies seize the chance to isolate and attack stragglers.

its hamstrings cut and missing a tail, this buffalo could not have gained much comfort from the noise whinnying through the flight feathers of the vultures. The birds began their feast on the open wounds, and it was some hours before before it died.

*(Below)* Lionesses chase and bring down their quarry but in the heat of the day they lack the motivation to finish it off. With

*(Above)*
A common sight in the game parks is the family
party of warthogs scampering through the
bush, tails vertical like radio antennae.
The warthog gets its English name from the
wart-like bump on its face.

*(Left)*
During the rainy season, tree frogs fill the
night with their mating calls.

*(Inset)*
A beetle's helmet moulded like eyes will
help to keep attackers away.

(*Opposite page*) Because it attacks maize, the vervet monkey is hunted as a pest by farmers. However, it is often used for laboratory experiments.

(*Left*) The Thornicroft's giraffe is distinguished by its broken up markings, brown forehead and fawn coloured flanks. Named after the British official who identified it, this sub-species of the giraffe family is unique to Zambia.

(*Below*) A hippo weighs as much as a family car and has to be immensely strong in order to support itself on dry land. It has adapted to water with its own peculiar abilities, such as changing its specific gravity so that it can sink and walk along the river bed.

## The Victoria Falls

Long before they were 'discovered' by David Livingstone, the Victoria Falls were known to the local people of the Zambezi as Mosi-Oa-Tunya, 'the smoke that thunders'. Livingstone exposed the Falls to the outside world and named them in deference to his queen. The Falls lie between Zambia and Zimbabwe, the Zambezi River separating the two countries.

Upstream the river can be two kilometres wide and very placid, but it suddenly gathers force, takes a headlong dive and plunges over a sheer basalt lip, 1,700 metres wide and 108 metres deep. The level of the water changes with the different seasons, with the result that the Falls can appear in many different moods. During the dry season, the flow of water over the Falls can be almost non-existent, but at the height of the floods, an unabated and torrential sheet of water cascades over the Falls, creating enormous clouds of spray which can be seen from 30 kilometres away.

The Victoria Falls are familiar to all the world, but few have seen much of the river beneath them. Sobek Expeditions run one and two day trips down this exciting river, which offers possibly the best white water rafting experience in the world. For the more adventurous tourist, there is a seven day expedition to make the 128 kilometre journey downstream through scores of rapids to the calm waters of Lake Kariba.

# *Birds*

*(Above)*
The Tawny Eagle is one of the 43 raptor species that
breed in Zambia, and is closely associated with the
presence of larger mammals.

*(Right)*
The African Fish Eagle is Zambia's national bird, dressed
in its multiracial plumage of black, brown and white.
Its haunting cry is broadcast on the radio, and it is depicted on
the Zambian flag and coat of arms as well as on postage stamps.
Fish eagles choose one mate for life, and partners are frequently
heard calling for each other down the length of a river valley.

Unlike many of her neighbours, Zambia is fortunate in that farming activities and urban sprawl have so far posed little threat to the well - being of birds: they are still to be found in tremendous variety.

*(Top row)* Carmine Bee-eater; Lilac-breasted Roller; the Bateleur Eagle (large photo) which takes its name from the French word meaning 'tightrope walker'. The bird rocks slowly from side to side in flight like the tightrope walker's balancing pole.

*(Middle row)* Common Sandpiper; Long Tailed Starling; Crowned Plover; Greater Blue-eared Starling

*(Bottom row)* Crested Barbet; Gaboon Nightjar; Black-collared Barbet; Crimson-breasted Boubou.

*(Opposite page)* The Malachite Kingfisher from its perch on a river bank reed, becomes a flash of colour as it dives to catch a tiny fish.

*(Previous page)* A Vulture flies in to join others feeding on the abandoned carcass of a dead lechwe. It may be as little as twenty minutes before nothing is left but skin and bones.

The African Spoonbill feeds in lagoons, sweeping the flattened end of its bill through the water in search of prey.

As the annual dry season advances, shorelines recede and many bodies of water dry up completely. In such an environment, birds must have good powers of flight to allow them to migrate as conditions change. African spoonbills fly in formation with strong wing beats.

(Right) The Crowned Crane is one of Zambia's most ornate birds: its size makes it conspicuous and its voice is memorable. Its strongholds are the dambos and flood plains of the Kafue, the Luangwa valley and Bangweulu.

(Far right)The cactus-like Euphorbia tree, whose thorn bearing stems contain a poisonous latex, is commonly used by birds of prey in which to build their nests. Here a Brown Snake Eagle takes flight from its prickly home.

(Left) The Pink-backed Pelican is associated with the major wetlands. The swamps of Mweru, Wantipa, Bangweulu, Leukanga, the Barotse flood plain and the Kafue flats harbour large concentrations of aquatic birds. One of the most exciting spectacles involving water birds are the fishing parties which take place as the dry season causes the waters to recede, trapping thousands of fish in the mud. Dozens of saddle bills, maribou and yellow billed storks all eat their fill, but when the pelicans descend, sometimes in their hundreds, the party is over. Pelicans are also at home in the air and flocks soar effortlessly on thermals, despite the fact that individuals can weigh up to seven kilogrammes.

A Great White Egret rests in the security of a drowned tree.
During the 20th century many dams have been
constructed and the reservoirs are now
frequented by a wide variety of water birds.

*(Opposite page)* The Goliath Heron stands 1.5 metres tall and
has a bill measuring up to 20 centimetres in length.
Its long legs allow it to feed in deeper water than other
Zambian herons.

# Missionaries

**Z**ambia, set deep in the interior of Africa, was one of the last regions of the continent to be explored by westerners. The first white people to arrive here were, by and large, Christian missionary pioneers, willing to suffer tremendous hardship and deprivation in order that they might carry out their Divine Mission. The list of their names is long, but in Zambia, that of David Livingstone is synonymous with lighting the way for early exploration by the West.

When Livingstone first encountered the Zambezi, he was excited to discover that it was an immense river which ran more than half way across Africa. He thought of the river as a useful highway along which Europeans could travel, bringing Christianity and 'civilisation' right to the heart of the continent. Although Livingstone's primary purpose was to spread the word of God, his desire to better the lives of the people he came across extended into secular activities as well. His approach is summarised in a letter he wrote from the bush, and it speaks for a generation of early missionaries:

"English races cannot compete in manual labour of any kind with the natives, but they can take a leading part in managing the land, improving the quality, creating the quantity, and extending the varieties of the production of the soil; and by taking a lead too in trade and in all public matters, the Englishman would be an unmixed advantage to everyone below and around him; for he would fill a place now practically vacant."

In Livingstone's wake followed equally enterprising pioneers such as Coillard and Moffat, who represented the Reformed churches, the Roman Catholic Bishop Du Pont - nicknamed Moto Moto - who established his faith firmly in the Bemba-speaking areas of the north, and Miss Mabel Shaw, whose Evangelical mission and orphanage remains a landmark of the Luapula Valley. They and many others are household names in Zambia today, for their efforts played a major role in promoting health, education and agriculture. Above all, they made it possible for Zambians even in those early days, to see themselves as part of a world stretching beyond the horizons their isolation had imposed on them.

The secret of the missionaries' success seems to have lain in their approach. Where Cecil Rhodes' British South Africa Company was merely pragmatic, they were radical. Where the Company - and subsequently the colonial government - left the indigenous people to their own culture, the missionaries intervened. They translated the Bible and taught the locals to read it, thus making their own work load lighter. For the same practical considerations, they taught arithmetic, to help with the running of the local community.

The early missionaries were striking for the level of their commitment. Malaria and dysentery were commonplace in many of the areas where they set up rural centres, and many died in the service of their God, happy in the knowledge that they were carrying out His will. They left behind miniature churches, schools and community houses, and to this day their remains consecrate the missions they founded. Even now, when most of the missionaries have gone and the churches in Zambia have to rely more on their own resources, the Church as a movement is one of the most notable voluntary organisations in the country.

Many missionaries developed an early sympathy for the Independence movement. They were not only among the first recognised and appointed representatives of African interests in the legislatures of the early and middle periods of colonial rule, but remained, as the fight for Independence intensified, the confidantes of many nationalists. With them, it was often possible to marry Christian principles with the moral tenets of the Zambian tradition of mutual support.

At the time of Independence in 1964, Zambia could only boast a handful of its own university graduates and Cambridge school certificate holders, but even so, most of them had sprung from the mission schools which, starting in the 1920s, grew in scope and strength through the 1930s and beyond. It was only after Zambia became independent that the burden of self support was eased, and today the missionaries and their Zambian confraternity continue to be involved in the tasks of healing, teaching and producing food. In so doing they have played a large part in grafting European culture onto the African continent: Jewish, Greek and Roman traditions are all abundantly evident in Zambian political and social life.

In town and country alike, Zambians continue to build churches, and the numerous religious programmes on radio and television are clear proof that though the forms of worship may have changed, the basic character of Christianity in the region remains the same.

When Livingstone emerged from the interior of Africa in 1856 he communicated to huge, cheering audiences in Britain his passionate belief in the future of Africa as a land of promise. He brought alive once again the evangelical fervour which had ended the slave trade. Of the missionaries who set out to follow Livingstone's example, most suffered terrible hardship and many died in the remote stations they had laboured to build. But the missionary movement survived, and much of Zambia's social, cultural and political life today stems from the schools and hospitals which are its legacy.

(Right and opposite) Some missionaries have been able to associate so intimately with the local culture that they have become custodians of the past. In what has amounted to a lifetime's work, the late Fr J.J. Corbeil of the White Fathers order established the Moto Moto Museum at Mbala in Northern Province. The museum, which contains a record of Bemba cultural history, is one of the finest ethnological collections on the African continent. It is named after the Bishop Dupont, who evangelised the area a century ago. "Moto Moto" was the nickname given to him by the locals.

(Below) The missionaries at Lubwe have from the outset been involved in social action. They and other missionaries have made a valuable contribution to improving the health and economy of the places in which they work.

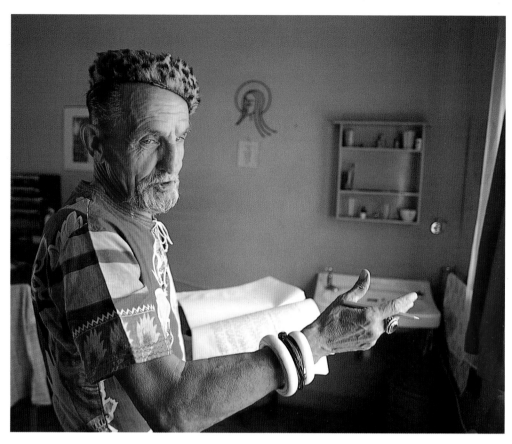

# Customs & Ceremony

It is commonly said there are over 70 tribes in Zambia, but while it is true that people living in the extremes of the country cannot understand each other's vernaculars, large areas are covered by mutually comprehensible dialects, and all of Zambia's languages can be classified into nine main groups, with a tenth introduced by the white invaders a century ago.

Change and decay in the tribal system has been brought about by the development in this century of the urban melting pots along the line of rail between Livingstone and the Copperbelt, and on the Copperbelt itself. This in turn has brought the realisation to many Zambians that a conscious effort must be made to preserve their traditions, customs and ceremonies, to defend traditional music against the onslaught of radio and record player, and to revive traditional spectacles.

Most of the ceremonies are invested with a special meaning. In many cases, they are designed to evoke memories of the transformation from childhood to adulthood. For centuries, virtually every tribe in Zambia has been conducting 'initiation' ceremonies for girls. These ceremonies, the details of which have always been a closely guarded secret from men, are generally conducted after puberty, and are intended to help the girls make the transition from childhood to womanhood, and to prepare them for the secrets of marriage.

By contrast, very few tribes in the country practice initiation ceremonies for boys. The notable exceptions are a few tribes in North-western and parts of Western Provinces which practice the Mukanda (circumcision ceremony). The ceremony, which lasts between six and nine months, is aimed at teaching young men how to look after their homes when they grow up. Like the girls' initiation ceremonies, outsiders are not allowed to witness the proceedings, and anyone straying to the Mukanda could be held captive and circumcised on the spot.

But there is another type of ceremony in Zambia which is usually an open spectacle that visitors can watch. These are the ceremonies which signify ancient times, when new kingdoms were being founded by great chiefs. The best known of these is the Kuomboka ceremony of the Lozi people in the Western Province. It dates back to more than 300 years ago when the Lozi broke away from the great Lunda Empire to come and settle in the upper regions of the Zambezi. There, in a vast plain, they found conditions ideal for settlement.

But although they loved the plains for their abundant fish, the plight brought by the annual floods could not be checked. One of the old legendary kings of the tribe, Litunga Mulambwa, organised his people to build clay mounds all along the valley to beat the floods, but it was impossible to defeat nature. So the Lozi stayed in the valley for nine months of the year, after which the floods made them flee to the uplands.

This is the annual migration, or 'Kuomboka' which has taken place every year since, for the lives of the Lozi are still dominated by the annual flooding of the Zambezi River whose banks they cultivate. Each year around March, the Litunga and his court move by barge out of Lealui, which is surrounded by floodwaters at this time of year. On the morning of the Kuomboka, summoned by the great maoma drums, thousands of canoes from all the villages in the flooded plain, carrying families and belongings, gather in the flood waters to accompany the Litunga's great barge, the Nalikwanda, with its crowd of privileged paddlers and drummers.

The Litunga himself wears a British Royal Navy admiral's uniform, originally given to one of his predecessors in 1902 by Edward VII in recognition of the treaties which were signed between King Lewanika and Queen Victoria. As the barge moves to Lumulunga followed by small canoes, the royal drums are sounded and great ululations fill the air. The journey takes about five hours, and before the barge approaches its destination, the Litunga changes into his admiral's uniform. On arrival, the Lozi ruler is welcomed by thousands of his subjects, and celebrations continue for another couple of days as tribal elders make their pilgrimage to Limulunga to greet their Litunga.

While the Kuomboka has taken place each year for centuries, other Zambian ceremonies which had died out have been revived in modern times. One of the best known is the Umutomboko of the Lunda people. Every year on July 29th, a bubbling throng of people converges on Mwansabombwe, a teeming community in Luapula Province.

The ceremony they attend is an annual reminder of the victories of Mwata (Chief) Kazembe, when his great kingdom migrated *en masse* into Luapula from the Congo. Legend has it that the dispersal began when the kingdom's paramount chief, Mwata Yamvo ordered his people to build a tower which would reach the sky so that they could bring him the sun and the moon. The tower collapsed during vain attempts to build it, killing many of the builders and causing many families to flee in terror.

Under the leadership of Kazembe, they travelled away across the river and into the east, conquering virtually all the tribes they encountered. Each time they conquered a people, they celebrated the victory which they called Umutomboko.

The two day ceremony is fabulous, mixed with ritual, semi-mystic performance, throbbing drums and lengthy speeches. It begins with women bringing tributes of beer and food to the Chief who, smeared with white powder, goes to pay homage to his ancestral spirits and is carried back to his palace to the sound of drums. On the second day, a goat is slaughtered before the Mutombuko dance led by the Chief. At the climax of the ceremony, the Chief takes a sword in his hand and points it in all directions, implying that there is nobody who could conquer him except God (when he points upwards). He then points down to indicate his place of rest when he dies.

War dances are performed during the ceremony, in tribute to the prowess and resilience of the dynasty which survived in Luapula for generations, and which successfully kept at bay attempts by the Portuguese to create links between their colonies on the east and west coast of Africa. To the Lunda people the Umutomboko is an emblem of what James Grady describes as "memories difficult to believe, detached moments crucial yet curious in the sum of our time. We lived them with stormy intensity, remember them with quiet awe: did we really play such a scene? Was there really such a time?"

Zambians today are taking an increasing interest in their own culture and history, and with Government backing are helping to stem the tide of modern life which washes away so much of deep emotional and traditional value.

*(Below)* Initiation ceremonies for girls are conducted by many Zambian peoples.

*(Right)* Mothers and daughters walk in procession at a ceremony in a Western Province village. The girl is carrying a cup of water on her head to her father. This requires some concentration, for if she spills a drop, she will have to undergo the entire initiation process again.

*(Opposite)* The ceremony is followed by traditional dancing.

## Kuomboka

The Kuomboka ceremony takes place towards the end of the rainy season when the water rises. Then the Litunga (Paramount Chief) and his court move from Lealui on the floodplain of the Zambezi to Limulunga on higher ground.

*(Right)* The Litunga leaves Lealui, and travels *(below)* aboard the Nalikwanda. During the journ he changes into his British admiral's uniform *(far right)*, a copy of the one given to King Lewanika by Edward the Seventh in 1902. When the Litunga dies, the uniform is buriedwith him and a new one made for his successor by the British Government.

*(Left)* A royal couple display a portrait of King Lewanika in the original admiral's uniform

The morning of Kuomboka brings hundreds of canoes carrying families and belongings from villages along the flooded plain to Lealui. There they join and follow the Nalikwanda to Limulunga. When the waters subside, the Litunga, his court and the villagers will return to the plain, and to fine grazing for their herds of cattle.

## Umutomboko

This schoolgirl is one of dozens who will carry the Umutomboko ceremony into the 21st century. She has coloured her face with blackboard chalk. Each year, Senior Chief Mwata Kazembe, 17th of the Lunda people of the Luapula, re-enacts the exploits of his ancestors when they migrated from Shaba in the early 18th century.

At the culmination of the ritual, eight bearers carry the
chief in his hammock to the arena near his palace
where he performs the Umutomboko, the royal dance
of conquest. The ceremony, which lasts for two days,
is full of intense dancing and gaiety.

At the climax, Kazembe points his ceremonial sword
in every direction to show his invincibility except
(as he points to the sky) against the Creator. At last, he
points to the ground, indicating his place of rest after
death. The sword is made by Lunda blacksmiths.
Mwata Kazembe's cotton skirt recalls an early king who
received gifts of cloth from Portuguese ambassadors.

## Lykumbi Lyamizi

*(Left)* The Luvale people hold an annual ceremony in which King Kayipu, named after a famous chief, leads the Makishi dancers representing figures from tribal mythology. The Makishi play an important part in the traditional rite of circumcision, Mukanda.

*(Right)* The late Senior Chief Ndugu wore for his enthronement a crown shaped like that of the great emperor Mwata Yamva, reminding the Luvale of their origins in the north.

*(Below)* The dancer Kutupoka offers blessings to the Chief.

*(Right)* This Likishi's mask and hat make him a caricature of the 19th century European empire builder.

*(Left)*  A Luvale traditional healer has her face powdered to show her beneficent spirituality. The Luvale have for centuries been great travellers and traders, and the beads and cowrie shells she wears recall their contacts with the Portuguese on the Angolan coast, five hundred years ago.

*(Following page)*  At the Mukunda, the boys' initiation enclosure, entertainment is provided by Chileya Chamukanda, the Fool, *(insert)* fly switch in hand, his calves girt with small gourd rattles. Makishi masks are made of wood and bark, decorated with paint and paper, while gloves, shirt and trousers are woven from dyed root fibres.

## Nc'wala

The Ngoni of the Eastern Province are descended from the Zulus who crossed the Zambezi from the south on 20th November 1835 (the date is known because of a total eclipse of the sun that day). For the next half century, they raided far and wide over the lands they discovered. They were finally defeated in 1898 by troops of the British Government brought in from Nyasaland, and their warlike festival of Nc'wala was suppressed until Independence. Now with leopard skin, knobkerrie and shield, Paramount Chief Mpezeni represents a tradition which - except for Mpezeni's praise singer - has all but lost its language. Today the Ngoni speak Chewa, the language of the people they conquered. A festival of First Fruits, very similar to Nc'wala, is held annually in Swaziland, far to the south, where other Ngoni, like the Ndebele in Zimbabwe, migrated long ago.

*(Top left)*
A fillet of cloth around an old warrior's head recalls the permanent headband of clay worked into the hair which Zulu headmen wore.

*(Top right)*
The hide of a noble animal, the leopard, designates royalty.

*(Bottom left)*
An ecstatic woman at the climax of the ceremony.

*(Bottom right)*
Headman Kampala, custodian of Ngoni history.

*(Right)*
The knobkerrie and cowhide shield are symbols of the Ngoni warrior past.